STRONG MENTAL MODELS
A VERY EFFECTIVE WAY TO MAKE INTELLIGENT DECISIONS

ANDREW L. HILTON

No part of this publication may be reproduced, distributed, or transmitted in any form or by any means, including photocopying, recording, or other electronic or mechanical methods, without the prior written permission of the publisher, except in the case of brief quotations embodied in reviews and certain other non-commercial uses permitted by copyright law.
Copyright © 2022 Andrew L. Hilton All rights reserved.
Table of contents.

Introduction

What Is Mental Strength? The Secret Of Becoming Mentally Strong
 The possibilities you have never known about the significance of mental strength are extremely thin, frankly. As one of my partners said: "These days, everybody is by all accounts discussing how you can turn into an intellectually tough individual on the off chance that you just pursue a studio or purchase a book". While a portion of these individuals has some significant exhortation, I understood that they frequently share the same things that you can undoubtedly find somewhere else. Further developing your psychological strength requires some work. However, the initial step of understanding what to do matters much comparably.

What is mental strength?

Mental sturdiness is one's capacity to defeat troubles, difficulties, and stress of day-to-day existence no matter what the conditions despite everything present one's most high effectiveness. Having mental strength will permit you to go with informed choices in answering a particular circumstance as opposed to responding to it. Assuming you're considering how it is conceivable, you will scarcely believe it. Intellectually tough individuals don't fear difficulties as they develop from them. Clear objectives, setting reasonable assumptions, and realizing their powers permit them to gain from their encounters.

It doesn't make any difference, so, all things considered, in your life, you are at this moment; if you can foster your psychological sturdiness, you can do as such. Like our build, everybody has specific inclinations concerning our mental and otherworldly capacities. Even though it tends to be simpler for certain individuals to develop muscle than it is for you or me, we can, in any case, create and turn out to be better individuals.

How might undesirable convictions be damaging?

With regards to a few of us not having the option to grow intellectually, it is because we will generally adhere to probably the most dangerous propensities. Laura G., a specialist, advises us that having ridiculous convictions about yourself, others, and the world is the thing that might be preventing you from turning into a more grounded person. Assuming you're continually zeroing in on your viewpoints on every one of the terrible things occurring to you, you will, before long, wind up lost in self-indulgence, which will keep you down.

Being answerable for your satisfaction can assist you with carrying on with your best life. Nonetheless, having unfortunate convictions about others can keep you from doing such. It isn't another person driving you crazy; you decide to respond with a particular goal. No one will give you enough life, and no one will hinder you from having it; you're the person who needs to fabricate it without any preparation. More than that, many of us have unfortunate convictions about the world. Difficult work won't generally be the solution to your inquiries; you ought to know what to deal with. Also, the possibility of reasonableness is artificial, and zeroing in on it will act as a reason for being harsh.

For what reason is it hard to surrender persistent vices?

It's very difficult to surrender your unfortunate convictions and move forward. Clutching your persistent vices will bring about you driving your joy further away. Consider it a safe place, which, can we be real for a moment, isn't simply agreeable. In great times, it is by and large simple to adhere to the positive convictions as a whole and appear to be an entirely resilient individual. Notwithstanding, when a bother occurs, it is only simpler to turn around to unfortunate things to do and allow them to hurt you much more.

Surrendering hurtful habits

Whether or not you need to foster your psychological strength or develop muscle, abandoning unfortunate behavior patterns isn't sufficient. You should likewise take a period and work to present sound convictions in your everyday practice. Some of the means that have shown to be helpful are care, reflection, and individual and expert turn of events. Center around your feelings, consider what you're feeling and why. Like this, you'll make certain to supplant your dangerous propensities for certain useful ones.

Survive your intense encounters

We know the inclination of needing to get away from difficult stretches; you've had it, and I've had it. Whether it is attempting to take on a lot of work or resting for such a large number of hours daily, there are numerous ways you should try not to confront what is happening. Despite how enticing it could be to do such, the choice is not gainful by any means over the long haul.

As we have referenced, intellectually resilient individuals can gain from their previous encounters, skip off them, and become better. You can't make any decisions from a predicament if you attempt to imagine it's not there. Furthermore, it won't ever disappear if you don't address it; all things being equal, it will come hurrying in multiple times more awful right when you get one calm second. Rather than causing it to seem like your battle isn't genuine, process it and push ahead.

Notwithstanding how hard you might think that further developing your psychological strength is, it is a continuous interaction instead of an objective. Each little step matters and you have perused this article can turn into the start of your self-revelation and care venture. You realize how generally, areas of strength intellectually are not confidential by any stretch of the imagination. The responses are directly before you, and you need to see them.

Chapter one How to Be Mentally Strong: Ways to Build Mental Toughness

How tough would you say you are?

Certain individuals appear to rapidly return from personal disappointments and mishaps, while others think it is considerably more troublesome.

When life wrecks you, will you be fast to get yourself and adjust to the conditions? Or, on the other hand, do you end up destroyed with little trust in your capacity to manage the test?

Assuming you end up in the last class, there is no real reason to stress. Fortunately, numerous pragmatic techniques exist for building mental strength; the quality can be learned and sharpened through training, discipline and difficult work.

Our versatility is, in many cases, tried when life conditions change suddenly and for the more terrible — like the passing of a friend or family member, the departure of a task, or the termination of a friendship. Such difficulties, be that as it may, present the potential chance to transcend and return significantly more grounded than you were previously.

Step-by-step instructions to Be Areas of Strength for intellectually

Mental strength is the limit of a person to manage stressors, tensions and difficulties and perform surprisingly well, regardless of the conditions where they track down themselves (Clough, 2002).

Developing mental fortitude is central to carrying on with your best life. Similarly, as we go to the exercise centre and lift loads to construct our actual muscles, we should likewise foster our emotional wellness using mental apparatuses and strategies.

Ideal psychological well-being assists us with carrying on with a daily existence that we love, have significant social associations, and have positive confidence. It likewise supports our capacity to face challenges, attempt new things, and adapt to the tough times that life throws us.

Mental strength includes growing everyday propensities that form mental muscle. It additionally includes surrendering unfortunate behaviour patterns that keep you down.

To be intellectually sound, we should develop our psychological fortitude! People who decide to focus on self-improvement create mental strength over the long run. Similar to seeing actual increases from working out and eating better, we should foster solid mental propensities, such as rehearsing appreciation, to gain psychological well-being.

In like manner, to see substantial additions, we should likewise surrender undesirable propensities, like eating low-quality food, and for mental additions, surrender unfortunate propensities, for example, feeling frustrated about oneself.

We are ready to turn out to be intellectually more grounded. The key is to continue rehearsing and practising your psychological muscles — as you would if you were attempting to develop actual fortitude!

On Building Flexibility and Mental Sturdiness

The expression "Flexibility," regularly utilized comparable to positive emotional well-being, is acquired from designing, where it alludes to the capacity of a substance or object to spring once more into shape ("Versatility," 2019). Similarly, a material item would require strength and adaptability to return quickly, so does an individual require these qualities to be intellectually versatile.

The American Mental Affiliation (2014) characterizes Mental Flexibility as:

"The most common way of adjusting great despite misfortune, injury, misfortune, dangers or even critical wellsprings of stress."

A similar idea, Mental Strength, alludes to the capacity to remain solid notwithstanding misfortune, to maintain your concentration and assurance regardless of the challenges you experience. An intellectually extreme individual considers challenge and difficulty to be an open door and not a danger and has the certainty and positive way to deal with taking what comes in their step (Strycharczyk, 2015).

To be intellectually intense, you should have some flexibility, yet not all versatile people are fundamentally intellectually extreme.

Assuming you consider it an illustration, strength would be the mountain, while mental sturdiness may be one of the procedures for getting over that mountain.

Strycharczyk (2015) finds it valuable to consider the distinction as far as the expression 'make due and flourish.' Versatility assists you with getting by, and mental durability assists you with thriving.

Mental durability starts when you consider what is crossing your thoughts without recognizing those contemplations or sentiments. Then, tracking down the assurance to bring out hopeful considerations about the circumstance within reach.

As per Strycharczyk and Clough (n.d.), strategies for creating mental sturdiness spin around five topics:

Positive Reasoning
Tension Control
Representation
Objective Setting
Attentional Control

Similarly, as with developing mental fortitude, creating mental strength requires mindfulness and responsibility. Intense people seem to accomplish more than the intellectually delicate and partake in a superior level of satisfaction.

Turner (2017) portrays four significant attributes of mental strength, which he calls the 4c's: Control, Responsibility, Challenge, and Certainty. One might have a couple of these characteristics, yet having the four characteristics in the mix is the way to progress.

Mental sturdiness can be estimated utilizing the MTQ48 Psychometric Instrument, built by Teacher Peter Clough of Manchester Metropolitan College. The MTQ48 Instrument is experimentally legitimate and solid in light of this 4C's structure, which estimates key parts of mental durability.

The 4 C's of Mental Strength: (Turner, 2017)

1. Control

The degree to which you believe you are in charge of your life, including your feelings and feeling of life reasons. The control part can be viewed as your confidence. Being high on the Control scale means feeling content just being yourself and having a fair idea of your identity.

You are ready to get a handle on your feelings — less inclined to uncover you are close to your home state to other people — and be less occupied by the feelings of others. Coming up short on the Control scale implies you could feel like occasions happen to you and that you have no control or impact over what occurs.

2. Responsibility

This is the degree of concentration and dependability. To be high on the Responsibility scale is to have the option to successfully define objectives and reliably accomplish them without getting diverted. A high Responsibility level shows that you are great at laying out schedules and propensities that develop achievement.

Falling short on the Responsibility scale shows that you might find it hard to lay out and focus on objectives or adjust schedules or propensities demonstrative of progress. You could likewise be quickly flustered by others or contending needs.

The Control and Responsibility scales address the Versatility part of the Psychological Durability definition. It seems OK because the capacity to return quickly from difficulties requires a feeling of realizing that you are in charge of your life and can roll out an improvement. It likewise requires centre and the capacity to lay out propensities and focuses on that will get you in the groove again to your picked way.

3. Challenge

This is the degree to which you are driven and versatile. To be high on the Test scale implies that you are headed to accomplish your own best, and you see difficulties, change, and affliction as any open doors as opposed to dangers; you are probably going to be adaptable and spry. Coming up short on the Test scale implies that you could consider the changing danger and keep away from novel or testing circumstances out of dread or disappointment.

4. Certainty

This is the degree to which you trust in your capacity to be useful and proficient; it is your self-conviction and the conviction that you can impact others. To be high on the Certainty scale is to accept that you will effectively finish responsibilities and to accept mishaps while keeping up with normal and, in any event, reinforcing your purpose. To be falling short on the

Certainty scale implies that you are effortlessly agitated by mishaps and do not accept that you are skilled or have any impact over others.

The Test and Certainty scales address the Certainty part of the Psychological Sturdiness definition. This addresses one's capacity to distinguish and take advantage of a chance and to consider circumstances to be chances to embrace and investigate. This appears to be legit since, supposing that you are positive about yourself and your capacities and connect effectively with others, you are bound to change over difficulties into fruitful results.

The most effective method to Assemble Strength in Grown-ups

As referenced before, mental strength is not a quality that individuals either have or do not have. Rather, it includes ways of behaving, considerations, and activities that can be learned and created in everybody. There might be a hereditary part to an individual's degree of mental versatility. However, it is surely something that can be based upon.

In a paper enlivened by the 2013 board of the Global Society for Horrendous Pressure Studies, Drs Southwick, Bonanno, Masten, Panter-Block, and Yehuda (2013) handled the absolute most squeezing momentum inquiries in flexibility research.

The specialists had various meanings of versatility, yet many of the definitions incorporated an idea of solid, versatile, and positive working in the repercussions of misfortune. They concurred that "versatility is a complicated development, and it could be characterized distinctively with regards to people, families, associations, social orders, and societies."

There was likewise an agreement that one's capacity to foster strength depends on many elements, including hereditary, formative, segment, social, monetary, and social factors; however that versatility can be developed in any case (Southwick et al., 2013).

Strength can be developed through resolve, discipline, and difficult work, and there are numerous techniques by which to do such. The key is to recognize ways that are probably going to function admirably for you as your very own feature unique methodology for developing flexibility.

Increment Mental Strength in Students

Like grown-ups, serious areas of strength for intellectually and teenagers can handle issues, return from disappointment, and adapt to life's difficulties and difficulties. They are versatile and have the mental fortitude and certainty of reaching their maximum capacity.

Creating mental strength in understudies is similarly as significant, possibly not more significant, as creating mental strength in grown-ups. As per Morin (2018), assisting jokes with creating mental strength requires a three-pronged methodology, showing them how to:

Supplant negative contemplations with positive, more practical considerations

Control their feelings, so their feelings do not control them.

Make a positive move.

However, numerous methodologies, discipline procedures, and training instruments assist youngsters with building their psychological muscles. The following are 10 techniques to assist understudies with fostering the strength they need to turn into an intellectually solid grown-up:

1. Show Explicit Abilities

As opposed to letting kids languish over their errors, discipline should be tied in with showing kids how to improve sometime later. Rather than discipline, use results that show valuable abilities, for example, critical thinking and motivation control.

2. Allow Your Youngster To commit Errors

Botches are a certain piece of life and learning. Show your youngster or understudy that this is and to such an extent that they ought not to be humiliated or embarrassed about misunderstanding something.

3. Show Your Youngster How to Foster Sound Self-Talk

It is critical to assist kids with fostering a practical and hopeful point of view and how to reexamine negative considerations when they emerge. Realizing this expertise right off the bat in life will assist them with continuing through troublesome times.

4. Urge Your Youngster to Overcome Fears Head-On

Empowering a kid to overcome their feelings of trepidation head-on will assist them with acquiring priceless certainty. One method for doing this is to help your youngster to step beyond their usual range of familiarity and overcome their feelings of trepidation each little move toward a turn while lauding and remunerating their endeavours.

5. Permit Your Youngster to Feel Awkward

It tends to be enticing to calm or safeguard your kid or understudy at whatever point they are battling, yet it is vital to permit them to lose or battle and demand that they are capable in any event when they would rather not be. Managing little battles all alone can assist youngsters with developing their psychological fortitude.

6. Assemble Character

Kids with areas of strength for a compass and worth framework will be better ready to pursue solid choices. You can help by imparting values like genuineness and empathy and setting out learning open doors that build up these qualities routinely.

7. Focus on Appreciation

Rehearsing appreciation is quite possibly the best thing you can accomplish for your emotional wellness, and it is the same for youngsters (for more, see our Gratitude Tree for Youngsters.) Appreciation assists us with keeping things in context, in any event, during the most difficult times. To bring up an intellectually solid kid, you ought to urge them to rehearse appreciation consistently.

8. Confirm Moral Obligation

Tolerating liability regarding your activities or mix-ups is essential for developing mental fortitude. Assuming your understudy is attempting to fault others for the way he/she thinks, feels or acts, steer them from pardons and consider clarifications.

9. Show Feeling Guideline Abilities

Rather than relieving or quieting your kid each time they are disturbed, show them how to manage awkward feelings alone so they do not grow up relying upon you to direct their mindset. Kids who grasp their scope of sentiments (see the Inclination Haggle) experience managing them are more ready to manage the good and less promising times of life.

10. Be A Good example of Mental Strength

There could be no greater method for showing a youngster than a visual demonstration. To support mental strength in your understudies or kids, you should exhibit mental strength. Show them that you focus on personal development in your life, and discuss your objectives and steps you take to develop further.

13 Methods for building and Further developing versatility

As we have noted, your degree of mental versatility is not something settled on upon entering the world — it tends to be worked on throughout a singular's life. Underneath, we will investigate various procedures and strategies used to work on mental flexibility.

Loot Whitley, PhD (2018), proposes three strength improving systems:

1. Expertise Securing

Procuring new abilities can significantly impact building strength, as it assists with fostering a feeling of dominance and capability — the two of which can be used during testing times, as well as increment one's confidence and capacity to issue settle.

Abilities to be mastered will rely upon the person. For instance, some could profit from further developing mental abilities, for example, working memory or specific consideration, which will assist with regular working. Others could profit from learning new side interests exercises through capability-based learning.

Getting new abilities inside a social scene gives the additional advantage of social help, which likewise develops flexibility.

2. Objective Setting

The capacity to foster objectives, noteworthy stages to accomplish those objectives, and to execute all assistance to foster self-control and mental flexibility. Objectives can be huge or little, connected with actual well-being, profound prosperity, vocation, money, otherworldliness, or anything else. Objectives that include expertise obtaining will have a twofold advantage—for instance, figuring out how to play an instrument or learning another dialect.

Some examination demonstrates that defining and making progress toward objectives past the individual, for example, strict contribution or chipping in for a purpose can be particularly valuable in building versatility. This might give a more profound feeling of inspiration and association, which can be significant during testing.

3. Controlled Openness

Controlled openness alludes to the steady openness to nervousness inciting circumstances and is utilized to assist people with defeating their feelings of dread. Research demonstrates that this can cultivate versatility, particularly when it includes expertise procurement and objective setting — a triple advantage.

Public talking, for instance, is a valuable fundamental ability yet something that brings out dread in many individuals. Individuals who fear public talking can put forth objectives, including controlled openness, to create or procure this specific ability. They can open themselves to a small crowd of a couple of individuals and logically increment their crowd size over the long haul.

The individual can start this activity plan, or it may be created by a specialist prepared for Mental Conduct Treatment. Effective endeavours can increment confidence and a feeling of independence and dominance, which can all be used amid misfortune.

4. Make associations.

Versatility can be fortified through our association with family, companions, and the local area. Sound associations with individuals who care about you and will pay attention to your concerns, offer help during troublesome times and can assist us with recovering expectations. Similarly, helping others in their period of scarcity can help us significantly and cultivate our feeling of strength.

5. Try not to consider emergencies to be impossible issues.

We cannot change the outside occasions around us, yet we have some control over our response to these occasions. Throughout everyday life, there will constantly be difficulties; however, it is essential to look past anything unpleasant circumstance you are confronted with and recollect that conditions will change. Consider the subtle manners by which you may begin feeling far improved as you manage the tough spot.

6. Acknowledge that change is a piece of living.

They say that the main thing steady in life is change. Because of troublesome conditions, certain objectives may, as of now, not be sensible or achievable. By tolerating what you cannot transform, it permits you to zero in on the things you actually do have command over.

However, it is vital to foster long-haul, 10,000-foot view objectives. It is fundamental to ensure they are reasonable. Making little, noteworthy advances makes our objectives feasible and assists us with consistently pursuing these objectives, making little "wins" en route. Attempt to achieve one little step towards your objective consistently.

7. Make unequivocal moves.

Rather than avoiding issues and stresses, wishing they would simply disappear, attempt to make an unequivocal move whenever the situation allows.

8. Search for open doors for self-disclosure.

In some cases, misfortune can bring about great learning and self-improvement. Living through a tough spot can expand our fearlessness and identity worth, fortify our connections, and show us an incredible arrangement. Many individuals who have encountered difficulty have likewise detailed an uplifted appreciation forever and developed otherworldliness.

9. Sustain a positive perspective on yourself.

Attempting to foster trust in yourself can be gainful in forestalling hardships and building flexibility. Having a positive perspective on yourself is significant concerning critical thinking and confidence in your senses.

10. Keep things in context.

At the point when challenges go crazy, consistently recollect that things could be more terrible; attempt to try not to make a huge deal about things—developing strength assists with keeping a drawn-out viewpoint while confronting troublesome or excruciating occasions.

11. Keep a confident viewpoint.

When we centre around what is negative about a circumstance and stay in an unfortunate state, we are less inclined to track down an answer. Attempt to keep a confident, hopeful viewpoint and expect a positive result rather than a negative one. Representation can be a useful procedure in this regard.

12. Taking care of yourself.

Taking care of oneself is a whole system for building strength and assists with keeping your psyche and body sufficiently solid to manage tough spots as they emerge. Dealing with yourself implies focusing on your necessities and sentiments and taking part in exercises that give you pleasure and unwinding. Ordinary activity is likewise a special type of taking care of oneself.

13. Extra approaches to reinforcing strength might be useful.

Strength building can seem to be various things to various individuals. Journaling, rehearsing appreciation, reflection, and other profound practices assist certain individuals with reestablishing trust and reinforcing their purpose.

The Way to Strength (APA)

The American Mental Affiliation (2014) characterizes flexibility as the most common way of adjusting despite the difficulty, injury, misfortune, dangers or huge wellsprings of stress — like family and relationship issues, serious medical conditions or work environment financial stressors. As such, "returning quickly" from troublesome encounters. Strength is not a characteristic that individuals either have or do not have.

It includes ways of behaving, considerations, and activities that can be learned and created in anybody.

Research has shown that strength is normal, not phenomenal and that individuals ordinarily exhibit versatility. A genuine illustration of this is the reaction of numerous Americans to the September 11 2001, militant psychological assaults and people's endeavours to remake their lives.

As the APA indicates, being strong does not imply that an individual does not encounter difficulties or misfortunes. Much close-to-home misery is normal in individuals who have managed hardships and injuries in their lives.

Factors in Strength

Many elements add to the flexibility, yet studies have shown that the essential component is having steady connections inside and beyond the family. Mindful connections, cherishing and offering support and consolation, assist with developing an individual's versatility.

The APA recommends a few extra factors that are related to strength, including:

The ability to make sensible disposition and significant stages to do them.

A positive self-view and trust in your assets and capacities.

Correspondence and critical thinking abilities.

The ability to oversee and control certain inclinations and motivations.

These are factors that individuals can create inside themselves.

Systems For Building Strength

With regards to creating versatility, methodologies will differ for every person. We respond diversely to horrendous and unpleasant life-altering situations, so a methodology that functions admirably for one individual won't work for another. For instance, some variety concerning how one could convey sentiments and manage misfortune might reflect social contrasts.

Gaining from Before

Investigating encounters and wellsprings of individual strength might give an understanding of which flexibility-building procedures will work for you. The following are a few directing inquiries from the American Brain science Affiliation that you can get some information about how you have responded to testing circumstances previously. Investigating the responses to these inquiries can assist you with creating future methodologies.

Think about the accompanying:

What kinds of occasions have generally been upsetting for me?

How have those occasions ordinarily impacted me?

Have I found it supportive to consider notable individuals in my day-to-day existence when I am upset?

To whom have I connected for help dealing with a horrendous or unpleasant experience?

What have I learned about myself and my collaborations with others during troublesome times?

Has it been useful for me to help another person through a comparative encounter?

Have I had the option to conquer obstructions, and assuming this is the case, how?

What has assisted me with a more confident outlook on what is in store?

Remaining Adaptable

A tough outlook is an adaptable mentality. As you experience upsetting conditions and occasions in your day-to-day existence, keeping up with adaptability and equilibrium in the accompanying ways is useful:

Allow yourself to encounter compelling feelings and acknowledge when you might have to set them to the side to work.

Step forward and make a move to manage your concerns and satisfy the needs of everyday living; in addition, know when to step back and rest/recharge yourself.

Invest energy with friends and family who proposition backing and consolation; sustain yourself.

Depend on others, yet in addition, know when to depend on yourself.

At times the help of loved ones is sufficiently not. Know when to look for help beyond your circle. Individuals frequently find it supportive of going to:

Self-improvement and local area support gatherings

Sharing encounters, feelings, data, and thoughts can give incredible solace to individuals who might feel like they are separated from everyone else during troublesome times.

Books and different distributions

Hearing from others who have effectively explored unfavourable circumstances like the one you are going through can give extraordinary inspiration and motivation to fostering an individual system.

Online assets

Assets and data are abundant on the web about managing injury and stress; simply be certain the data comes from a legitimate source.

An authorized emotional wellness proficient

For the overwhelming majority, the above ideas might be adequate to develop flexibility. However, sometimes, it is ideal to look for professional assistance on the off chance that you feel like you cannot work in your everyday existence because of awful or other unpleasant life-altering situations.

Forging ahead with your Excursion

To summarise the APA's central matters, a helpful illustration of strength includes taking an excursion on a kayak. On a boating trip, you can experience a wide range of waters — rapids, slow water, shallow water and a wide range of insane turns.

Like everyday life, these changing conditions influence your contemplations, state of mind, and the manners by which you will explore yourself. Every day, as in going down a stream, it assists with having previous experience and information from which to draw. Your process ought to be directed by a procedure that will probably function admirably for you.

Other significant perspectives remember certainty and conviction for your capacities to explore the occasionally rough waters and maybe having confided in allies to go with and support you on the ride.

The Strength Manufacturer Program

The Versatility Manufacturer Program for Youngsters and Teenagers — Improving Social Skill and Self-Guideline is a creative program intended to increment flexibility in youth. The book depends on a 12-week versatility-based bunch treatment program and applies Mental Conduct Hypothesis and methodologies.

The program frames 30 gathering meetings that work on confidence, restraint, certainty and methods for dealing with hardship or stress (Karapetian Alvord, Zucker, Johnson Grados, 2011).

Key capabilities tended to in every meeting incorporate mindfulness, adaptable reasoning, and social ability. Through conversation and active strategies, for example, pretending, bunch individuals learn about outrage/uneasiness on the board, critical thinking, individual space mindfulness, self-talk, fellowship abilities, and other fundamental points relating to social and individual prosperity.

These gathering exercises assist with creating explicit defensive elements related to flexibility.

The program incorporates unwinding procedures like representation, quiet breathing, moderate muscle unwinding, and yoga to upgrade self-guideline. To apply their learnings to the rest of the world, the program doles out schoolwork, local area field trips, and a parent's inclusion part.

Flexibility Developer Program is creative, thoroughly examined, sequenced and organized, and offers a well-organized bunch system, substantial enough for fledglings. This is an outstanding choice if you are searching for a definite program to show your kid or understudy how to be strong.

The Acknowledging Versatility Masterclass

If you are a mentor, educator or guide and it is your obsession to help other people become stronger, then the Acknowledging Strength Masterclass© is the exact thing you want.

Comprising six modules incorporating positive brain science, flexibility, consideration, contemplations, activity and inspiration, this complete web-based course will effectively give you key mental ideas for anybody new to the field.

Endless supply of the independent course, you will be granted a testament and can utilize the broad library of devices, worksheets, recordings, and introductions to instruct flexibility.

Working on Mental Endurance

"Endurance" is characterized by The Oxford Word reference as the capacity to support delayed physical or mental exertion ("Endurance," 2019).
Mental endurance is the central attribute that empowers us to get through life's misfortunes. It is fundamental for enduring long-haul difficulties or random battles, concerns or injuries and is evolved by training and reiteration.
Mental endurance requires strength, diligence, and fixation (Walkaden, 2016).
Mental endurance resembles an advanced cross-breed among coarseness and versatility.
(Walkaden, 2016).
Frequently, when we discuss endurance, we reference top competitors and sports groups, as physical and mental endurance is pivotal for this sort of exhibition. In any case, everybody can profit from expanded mental endurance, not simply competitors. Albeit nobody assembles mental endurance short-term, underneath Corb (n.d.) offers 5 ways to fabricate your psychological endurance over the long run:
1. Think Decidedly
Self-assurance and faith in one's capacity to perform and pursue choices are one of the main qualities of a solid psyche. Preparing yourself to think hopefully and find what is going on will unquestionably assist with building mental endurance over the long haul.
2. Use Perception
Representation is a magnificent apparatus for overseeing Pressure, overpowering circumstances, and execution nervousness. Shut your eyes and envision a period when you prevailed experiencing the same thing. This incorporates recollecting the inclination that went with that accomplishment and the visual.

3. Plan for Misfortunes

Life unquestionably does not generally go how we trusted or arranged that it would. It is vital to re-focus and recover after a difficulty instead of harp on the misfortune or incident. We have zero control over the outer occasions that occur around us; however, we have some control over what we do a while later. Setting up an arrangement to assist you with managing when things do not work out as expected is smart.

4. Oversee Pressure

Our capacity to oversee Pressure assumes a huge part in our capacity to construct mental endurance. However, not all Pressure is terrible — positive Pressure (fervour) can be a propelling component — it significantly affects our bodies.

Valuable methods for overseeing Pressure incorporate contemplation and moderate muscle unwinding. You must be in charge of your psychological state and how you will deal with the stressor within reach.

5. Get More Rest

No mystery getting sufficient rest is essential to our physical and mental working in ordinary day-to-day existence. Adequate rest can assist with on-the-spot navigation and response time. An adequate measure of rest is supposed to be seven to nine hours or more if you perform high-stress physical and mental exercises.

Upgrading Strength Locally

Local area versatility is the supported capacity of a local area to use accessible assets (energy, correspondence, transportation, food, and the likes) to answer, endure, and recuperate from unfriendly circumstances (for example, financial breakdown to devastating worldwide dangers) (Bosher, L. and Chmutina, K., 2017).

Effective variation in consequence of a debacle guarantees that a local area can return to ordinary life as easily as expected. Local area transformation is generally subject to populace well-being, working, and personal satisfaction (Norris, Stevens, Pfefferbaum, Wyche, and Pfefferbaum, 2007).

Similar to when confronted with any issue, a local area should devise a strategy to meet up and modify after a calamity. The following are the key parts fundamental for a local area to fabricate aggregate flexibility after a misfortune:

Diminish hazard and asset disparities
Connect with nearby individuals in relief
Make authoritative linkages
Help and safeguard social backings.
Plan for not having an arrangement, which requires adaptability, decision-making abilities, and confided in wellsprings of data that capability even with questions.

What Constructs Strong Connections?

Flexibility is a vital part of any relationship. Connections require progressing consideration and development, particularly during seasons of difficulty. Have you considered what makes a few companionships or heartfelt connections bound to get by more than others? Underneath, Everly (2018) proposes specific variables which appear to encourage flexibility in connections and improve their probability of endurance.

Seven Attributes of Profoundly Strong Connections

1. Dynamic Good faith

Dynamic good faith is not simply trusting that things will end up great; rather, it is accepting that things will end up great and afterwards making a move that will prompt an improved result. In a relationship, this implies consent to keep away from basic, harmful, critical remarks and to cooperate in outfitting the force of an unavoidable positive outcome.

2. Genuineness, Honesty, Tolerating Liability regarding One's Activities, and the Readiness to Excuse

When we focus on tolerating liability regarding our activities, being faithful to and pardoning one another (and ourselves), we will undoubtedly develop strength inside our connections. This incorporates the familiar proverb that genuineness is the smartest idea, regardless of the result and outcomes.

3. Conclusiveness

This implies daring to make a move, in any event, when the activity is disagreeable or incites uneasiness in a relationship. Definitive activity some of the time implies leaving a toxic relationship or one that is not serving you well any longer, frequently advancing one's very own strength.

4. Constancy

Constancy is to persist, particularly despite demoralization, mishaps, and disappointments. It is significant to see someone recall that there will constantly be back-and-forth movements, great times, and difficult situations.

5. Poise

Following connections, the capacity to control driving forces, oppose enticements and defer delight are significant characteristics. Restraint assists one with staying away from rehearses that will adversely affect their relationship while advancing sound practices, particularly notwithstanding difficulty.

6. Relational Connectedness Through Legitimate Correspondence

The feeling of "having a place" and connectedness in a relationship is kept up with and sharpened through open, legitimate correspondence. Intermittently the most troublesome discussions to have are the main ones.

7. Common sense

Present-mindedness has numerous positive ramifications for the individual, which is likewise valid for accomplices in a relationship. Present-disapproved of mindfulness inside a relationship prompts a quiet, non-critical reasoning style and open correspondence. Good judgment empowers cooperative reasoning and receptiveness to new arrangements instead of destroying them and projecting fault.

These are only a portion of the qualities that foresee versatility in a relationship and improve the probability of a relationship bouncing back after tough spots.

How, In all actuality, do Individuals Figure out how to Become Versatile forever?

If you have any desire to become versatile forever, it is ideal, to begin with building your flexibility right now! Practice and obligation to the procedures and tips examined above will increment your capacity to return quickly and adjust whenever life has given you difficulties over the long haul.

The silver lining to encountering unfriendly life-altering situations is that the more you can utilize your flexibility muscle, the better you will want to return the next time life confuses you!

Contextual investigation Showing Ways Of building flexibility

In this review, Lipaz Shamoa-Nir (2014) presents a depiction of building hierarchical and individual versatility at three degrees of foundation: the board, staff, and understudies of a multi-social school. To do this, the school used three system models: the contact speculation model, the joint activities model, and the hypothetical model.

The review examines the intricacies of developing this multi-layered system for further developing correspondence between a fundamentally different gathering of understudies with contradicting political and social perspectives. The understudies are outsiders living under constant danger of social and financial emergency, with Pressure and clashes inside and remotely.

Each establishment level should add to creating survival techniques for emergencies and everyday reality. For personnel, this incorporates building a program that considers the qualities and shortcomings of understudies from social minority gatherings. For understudies, this incorporates social tasks that express their social and public variety.

In particular, the cycle requires authority from the executives-centred arrangements and exercises expected to impart a feeling of certainty and conviction at all levels of the association.

A few critically important points from the contextual analysis are that although cycles for building strength might require quite a long while, they can be advanced quickly by changes or emergencies that emerge; and that while parts of flexibility are implicit routine circumstances, the majority of them are just tried in emergency circumstances.

Each individual fosters their extraordinary adapting style, the proposed complex strength model references these six factors that involve each style:

Convictions and Values
Influence
Social
Creative mind
Perception
Physiology

Ultimately, the contextual investigation might apply to different associations or networks during or post-struggle.

Instructions to Get a Superior, More grounded and More Sure Psyche

Certainty is one of the 4C's of mental sturdiness! Sustaining a positive self-view and creating trust in your capacity to take care of issues and pay attention to your gut feelings is one of the fundamental elements in building versatility. So how would we develop more certain care?

The following are 10 dependable ways that you can start constructing your certainty (Scaffolds, 2017):

1. Finish Things

Certainty and achievement remain closely connected. Achieving objectives and, surprisingly, making little strides towards your objectives can assist with building your confidence and trust in your capacities.

2. Screen Your Advancement

While pursuing an objective, huge or small, it means quite a bit to separate it into more modest, sensible advances. In doing so, one will find it simpler to screen their advancement and construct certainty as they see the improvement occurring progressively. It assists with evaluating your objectives and the significant stages towards those objectives.

3. Make the best choice

Profoundly sure, individuals will more often than not live by a worthy framework and pursue choices in light of that esteem framework, even when it is not really to their greatest advantage. When your choices are lined up with your most noteworthy self, it can develop a more sure brain.

4. Work out

Practice helps your actual body as well as your brain also. Mental advantages of activity incorporate better concentration, memory maintenance, and stress and tension administration. Practice is additionally said to forestall and support sadness. Certainty from practising comes from the physical, apparent advantages, yet additionally from the psychological advantages.

5. Be Valiant

To be dauntless in chasing your fantasies and objectives requires a degree of certainty. Alternately, testing yourself by making a plunge into things that alarm you will assist with building your certainty. Frequently, when we put forth major objectives for ourselves, it is not difficult to get overpowered and be disappointed. On these occasions, it is critical to get together your mental fortitude and continue onward mindfully.

6. Support Yourself

To support yourself when somebody lets you know that you cannot achieve something is a compelling method for fostering your certainty. Time and again, we might wind up trusting the cynics, as they are repeating oneself uncertainty we might be hearing in our minds. To sustain a positive self-view is to supplant those negative contemplations with positive ones. Attempt to do such also when somebody does not trust in you.

7. See everything through to completion

Finishing what you say will not just assist with gaining the appreciation of others but also regard for and trust in yourself. Fostering your completion abilities will likewise assist you with achieving your objectives and reasonably fortify your connections.

8. Think Long haul

Customarily, we exchange long-haul joy for more prompt delight. We can develop our certainty by pursuing penances and choices in light of long-haul objectives instead of transient solaces. Tracking down the discipline to do so will get more prominent bliss over the long haul and a higher probability of accomplishing the objectives you have set for yourself.

9. Try not to Tend to think about Others' Thought process

It is not difficult to fall into the snare of considering what others might think about you. However, others' thought processes must make no difference in chasing your fantasies. Construct your certainty by trusting in yourself and proceeding to push ahead, in any event, when others probably will not concur with you.

10. Accomplish A greater amount of What Fulfills You

When we get some margin for taking care of ourselves and doing the things that give us pleasure, it assists with improving our lives and turns us into the best version of ourselves. Certainty comes when we are lined up with our most elevated selves and glad for it.

A Bring back Home Message.

At the base of a significant number of these instruments and techniques for building your psychological wellness are Mindfulness and Acknowledgment. To upgrade and refine our current mental strength, we should know where we are at and acknowledge that this is where we are at. Really at that time, might we start to move toward a more grounded, better mental state?

Another important point is that you have zero control over everything that happens to you, yet you have some control over how you respond to what occurs. In these cases, your psyche can be your greatest resource or worst adversary. When you figure out how to prepare it well, you can return from tough spots and achieve mind-blowing accomplishments.

You should be in great psychological well-being to encounter more noteworthy in general life fulfilment. Mental wellness incorporates strength, sturdiness, and versatility. Building these muscles might be exceptionally difficult and could require long periods of exertion and responsibility. Nevertheless, the advantages of being intellectually fit and tough will be found in all parts of your life.

Improved execution, better connections, and a more special feeling of prosperity can be in every way accomplished by creating sound mental propensities while surrendering undesirable mental propensities.

We can all work on our emotional well-being by carrying out these systems and focusing on the interaction for as long as possible.

Chapter 2

Things Intellectually Tough Individuals Don't Do

Developing mental fortitude assists individuals with arriving at their objectives and becoming their best selves.

Perceiving and supplanting the undesirable considerations, ways of behaving, and sentiments that harm one's earnest attempts is vital to developing mental fortitude.

Intellectually challenging individuals don't loathe others. Their meaning of accomplishment spurs them.

We frequently hear counsel like, "Think positive, and beneficial things will occur," or, "Attempt your hardest, and in the long run, everything will pan out." While such helpful tidbits unquestionably have merit, these good-natured ideas won't assist you with arriving at your objectives, assuming you're at the same time taking part in the unfortunate way of behaving. Perceiving and supplanting the undesirable considerations, ways of acting, and sentiments that might be subverting your earnest attempts is the way to developing mental fortitude.

Take a stab at contrasting mental strength with actual strength. While a jock keeps up with his physical make-up with positive routines, such as going to the rec center, that muscle head should dispose of unfortunate things, such as eating low-quality food. An activity routine won't be compelling in building fit muscle except if undesirable dietary patterns are likewise wiped out.

Also, building mental muscles requires arduous work, devotion, and exercise. As well as taking on sound propensities, keeping away from hindering dispositions — like pessimistic considerations, inefficient ways of behaving, and pointless feelings — is also fundamental.

Whether you're dealing with turning into a quieter parent or trying to turn into a world-class competitor, developing mental fortitude will assist you with arriving at your objectives. Figure out how to recognize the regular entanglements you're inclined to and practice practices that will help you become the best version of yourself.

Here are the few things intellectually formidable individuals don't do:

Sit around idly, Feeling frustrated about Themselves.

Many of life's concerns and distresses are inescapable, yet it is a decision to feel frustrated about yourself. Whether you're battling to cover your bills or managing unexplained medical issues, enjoying self-indulgence won't fix your concerns. If you're inclined to feel frustrated about yourself while the going gets unpleasant, train your cerebrum to trade self-indulgence for appreciation. Intellectually formidable individuals don't sit around idly contemplating the issue; all things being equal, they center around making an answer.

Mental Stunts That Will Assist You With halting Feeling frustrated about YourselfSelf

The difficulty is unavoidable. Be that as it may, self-indulgence is discretionary.

The difficulty is unavoidable whether a financial slump has negatively affected your ledger or you're managing an ongoing medical problem that disrupts your day-to-day existence. Be that as it may, how you deal with life's unavoidable difficulties depends on you.

You can either create the best of an extreme circumstance or dive in your heels and enjoy some excessive self-indulgence. In any case, deciding to feel frustrated about yourself has a few severe outcomes.

It will deplete you of the psychological strength you should be your best. Moreover, it could keep you caught in an unfortunate pattern of wretchedness.

Trouble is an ordinary, solid inclination. You are feeling a piece sorrowful can assist you regarding something that you've lost. Furthermore, permitting yourself to feel terrible for some time is critical to recuperating a profound injury.

However, self-indulgence is unique. It goes past solid trouble. When you feel frustrated about yourself, you'll misrepresent your incident and experience a feeling of sadness and powerlessness.

You could begin imagining that your life won't ever be outstanding from this point onward. Also, you could presume that nobody might assist you with feeling much improved. This perspective is pointless.

Self-indulgence creates an undesirable cycle. You'll develop to accept any work you put into changing your life will be futile. You won't make any move like this, and you'll remain caught in a dim spot.

Whether you need to forestall self-indulgence, or you've proactively begun feeling frustrated about yourself and need to stop, these two mental stunts will stop the pity party:

At the point when you wind up amidst a pity party, you'll be enticed to squander your energy, remaining stuck there. Instead of fixing your concerns, you'll invest energy in demanding potential arrangements that won't work.

You'll likely end up grumbling about the shamefulness of your circumstances with an end goal to get others to go to your pity party. And keeping in mind that your grievances might assist you with acquiring some brief compassion, your endeavors will ultimately unleash destruction on your public activity.

Sympathizing with individuals around you isn't exactly a holding movement. Nobody at any point says, "What I truly like about her is that she feels frustrated about herself." And as you repulse individuals, you'll be bound to fall further into self-indulgence.

So it's essential to change your way of behaving. Do things that make it harder to enjoy your horrendous contemplations.

This might include getting up off the lounge chair and getting going. Active work can do wonders for your psychological and profound state. So take a walk, take a run, or begin cleaning the house. Moving your body can move your outlook.

You could likewise accomplish something kind for other people. Volunteer for a cause, help a companion, or track down somebody out of luck. Kind demonstrations remind you of the amount you can provide for other people and keeps you from remaining fixed on what you figure others ought to accomplish for you.

While self-indulgence makes you think, "I merit better," appreciation is tied to thinking, "I have more than I merit." And significantly altering how you feel can avoid self-indulgence while working on your life in many ways.

Concentrating on show appreciation offers many advantages, from better rest and further well-being to more mental strength and flexibility to push.

There are numerous ways of rehearsing appreciation. You could write in an appreciation diary each night. Or, on the other hand, you could practice it regularly to contemplate three things you're thankful for each time you're enticed to whine about how terrible your life is.

The key is to track down an appreciation technique that works for you. When you perceive all, you must be grateful for it, and you'll never again be enticed to set up a pity party.

Surrendering self-indulgence will make you intellectually more grounded. Also, the more grounded you become, the simpler it is to keep self-indulgence under control.

Declining to feel frustrated about yourself guarantees that you won't burn through the necessary time and valuable energy wishing things were unique. All things being equal, you'll be prepared to make the positive move you want to take care of issues, adapt to your uneasiness, and foster a better standpoint.

The Blame Game.

Faulting others for our concerns and circumstances can vary entice. Thinking things like, "My mother by marriage causes me to regret myself," genuinely gives others control over us. Reclaim your power by tolerating entire liability regarding your thought process, feelings, and actions. Engaging yourself is fundamental to developing mental fortitude and making the sort of everyday routine you need to experience.
Quit Playing "Attempt at finger pointing."
Tracking down Arrangements, Not Issue
Envision you're going up a significant task. The cutoff time is approaching. However, the work will be postponed, and your supervisor needs to know why.
You and your group are approached to account for yourselves, and in no time, an "attempt at finger-pointing" starts as you attempt to identify who's to blame and why the conversation goes around.
Fooling around pointing fingers instead of searching for arrangements is a specific event, yet it's nowhere near helpful.
Here, we investigate what an attempt at finger-pointing is, how to stop it whenever it's begun, and how you can keep away from it in any case.
What Is an attempt at finger-pointing?
When something turns out badly, and we feel compromised, it's normal to need to shield ourselves against any repercussions. We could find ourselves scapegoating or attempting to move the fault somewhere else.
We might attempt to limit any association with an issue, expecting that assuming a sense of ownership with blunders or errors could hurt our vocations or make us look terrible.
Be that as it may, this approach addresses nothing. Moving the fault won't assist you with fulfilling that time constraint, and it doesn't fix the issue that created the setback.

Sometimes, it's pretty clear when a group is playing an attempt at finger-pointing. In any case, it can also occur in additional unpretentious ways.

Here are a few admonition signs to look out for:

Rejection: a couple of group members are routinely barred or underestimated. They might be "more vulnerable" than the others (either in character or position) or missing from the conversation.

"Blame shifting": colleagues track down issues inside the gathering. For instance, "Jack should take a look at those figures before the show."

Refusal: individuals reject obligation or concoct pardons. They might offer remarks, for example, "That isn't anything to do with me, nobody showed that data to me!"

Pessimism: no arrangement is recognized to fix the main thing needing attention. Individuals become focused on tracking down the issue. They battle to push ahead and spotlight the negative.

The Effect of Fault

Accusing others can unfavorably affect resolve and execution. Colleagues might feel disparaged or embarrassed, assuming they're pinpointed for fault - particularly on the off chance that it's not their shortcoming. (Our article, Managing Out of line Analysis, offers counsel on the best way to answer assuming you're singled out along these lines.)

A fault culture may likewise prompt people or groups to be scapegoated when the genuine issue might lie somewhere else or have various causes. It's more straightforward to fault somebody in one more office or work than to blame somebody you sit with each day.

Over the long run, this scapegoating might try and sustain inclination or bias or lead to allegations of segregation. Additionally, it can harm the honesty of colleagues who witness it, particularly assuming they never really stop it.

"Shifting responsibility elsewhere" can drain entrust with clients and providers and give your association a terrible name. Discussions such as, "Indeed, that is the money group's shortcoming, not our own, so I can't help you," cause the entire organization to appear clumsy.

Fault can likewise stunt imagination and advancement inside your association - assuming that individuals are hesitant to attempt new circumstances if they don't pan out, this can lessen group and company executives in the more extended term.

At last, a few people might be inclined to tolerate fault where it isn't justified. A defensive director, for instance, may "take the rap" for another person's error. Or on the other hand, a person who's profoundly self-basic might see everything as their issue, in any event, when it isn't.

Caution:

Staying away from an attempt at finger-pointing doesn't imply "allowing things to go unaddressed" or trusting that a circumstance will sort itself out. For instance, on the off chance that a person's messy work brings about issues, absence of exertion, or lacking meticulousness, suitably tending to them is significant. Peruse our article, Managing Terrible showing, to more deeply study this.

The inability to handle issues like these could cause disdain in the remainder of the group, permit a similar problem to happen again, or imply that others must make up for their partner's weaknesses.

The most effective method to Keep away from an attempt at finger pointing

Pointing the finger of fault tackles nothing. Cooperate to track down an answer, all things being equal.

Defining explicit assumptions and limits for your team is significant to forestall a fault culture.

The accompanying activities can assist you with staying away from the circumstance emerging in any case:

Lay out explicit liabilities and responsibilities. When individuals know their obligations precisely, it's harder to fault others when things turn out badly, and it isn't very sure to turn out badly.

By empowering individual responsibility and not continuously fussing over it, your colleagues will feel pride over their errands. You really might consider drawing up a group contract that sets out everybody's assumptions and goals recorded as a hard copy.

Encourage transparency. An open and cooperative group will be better furnished to manage likely issues before they go crazy. Request regular contributions from your group at gatherings (or separately, for individuals who are less open to making some noise in communities).

Keep an eye out for mindless obedience, where individuals become careful about bringing up troublesome issues because of a paranoid fear of disturbing the state of affairs.

Sustain your ability to understand individuals on a profound level and with sympathy. Regardless of whether a partner is to blame, there might be different variables to consider. Maybe they are overextended, or a family crisis drove them to neglect something significant.

Intend to offer help rather than analysis. If a colleague commits an error or neglects to follow through on an errand, they might require instruction, tutoring, or preparation on a particular expertise.

Accept there is an illustration to be learned and agree to learn it.

This is presumably quite possibly the primary step. Except if you're genuinely able to get familiar with the illustration, regardless of whether it feels awkward now and again, you can never push ahead. Agree to see what is happening as something that can assist you with developing.

Concede that you could have made the issue.

Caution: This expects you to stop looking for someone else to take the blame immediately! Think about how conceivable it is that you somehow added to your ongoing circumstance. This doesn't mean no other person had an influence; it simply implies maybe you did, too.

Take some alone time and audit what is happening.

I'm sure you've done this on different occasions. Now is the ideal time to diversely make it happen. Attempt to see what is going on according to an alternate point of view. Get a goal and see it from another person's eyes. Is there another method for interpreting what occurred and how everything worked out?

This expects you to be genuinely legitimate with yourself about your decisions and activities. Assuming you're willing to adjust your viewpoint, you may quickly see what example should be realized and how to gain proficiency with the illustration.

Relinquish your connection to the issue.

Attempting to control the issue — your chief, your life partner, or your conditions — will keep you more appended to it. The more you "siphon" onto a case, the more it "leeches" right back on you.

You will always be unable to see the example or the arrangement if you harp on every one of the little insights concerning what appears to be off-base. Giving up could come in many structures: seeing the positive qualities in the individual who seems to be troublesome, tolerating what is happening for what it is, or visiting the opposite side of the story.

Any time we let go of our connection to what turned out badly or what ought to have occurred, we make the chance of development clear the way for other positive outcomes.

My undisputed top choices were stages three and four. When I surveyed my marriage from an outsider's viewpoint, I saw everything I might have improved. After that second, I conceded the job I played, excused myself, and was finally ready to push ahead.

Dropping fault permitted me to give up and continue.

Stopping attempts at finger-pointing and learning life illustrations has permitted me to be in cherishing, equivalent, and, the best part, loosen up relationships. It's allowed me to construct my fantasy vocation. It's additionally permitted me to take a gander at every obstruction I'm confronting and track down something positive to detract from it.

On the off chance that you're having an issue, there is an example to be learned. Become familiar with the model then you get to push ahead. That is the way a game ought to work!

Avoid Change.

Even though we feel most secure when we stay inside our usual ranges of familiarity, staying away from new provokes fills in as the most significant impediment to carrying on with a complete and prosperous life. Figuring out how to perceive when you keep away from change in light of the uneasiness engaged with experimenting could be the most crucial phase in a long excursion toward working on your life. The more you work on enduring the awkward sentiments related to change — whether it includes taking on a new position or leaving an unfortunate relationship — the more sure you'll become in your capacity to make your future.

Why do You have a fear of change and Ways Of conquering It?

Everybody encounters a degree of dread of progress. That is the reason safe places exist. You're in good company in these sentiments encompassing change. Neuroscience has shown that vulnerability feels like disappointment in our minds. That is why so many individuals would prefer to keep away from instability due to how awkward the related sentiments can be.

While it's normal to feel that change is startling, specific individuals might be managing something more serious. Something more is called metathesiophobia, and it's such a great apprehension about evolution that it tends to deaden and is extremely hard to live with.

We will take a gander at fearing change, the typical side effects of metathesiophobia, how to live with the anxiety toward change, and strategies to defeat such sentiments.

What is Dread of Progress?

Marked metathesiophobia, this degree of dreading change causes dynamic ridiculous, and severe tension while confronting new circumstances or encounters.

Expected Side effects of metathesiophobia

The individuals who have metathesiophobia may have insight:

Uneasiness

Discouragement

Weariness

Torment

Stress

Instances of a Feeling of dread toward change

There is a wide range of life encounters where individuals experience the ill effects of apprehension about change instead of deciding to roll out the improvement; in any event, pursuing the difference is the better choice.

For instance, an individual might decide to remain in a toxic relationship since they are terrified of the option of being single or going on dates to track down another accomplice.

One more model is when individuals wait in positions that make them hopeless or feel unsatisfied because they are terrified to begin a new post.

As may be obvious, the ideal arrangement is to continue and have a go at a novel, new thing. Be that as it may, when you're trapped in a circumstance and have metathesiophobia, you can't see so obviously.

For what reason Do We Dread Change?

We dread change since it implies that results are obscure. Our minds are intended to discover a sense of harmony in knowing. When we don't know what will occur, we makeup situations and, thus, create stress.

People find it hard to continue when something known concludes. The apprehension about disappointment likewise becomes possibly the essential factor in making anxiety toward change. If we don't have the foggiest idea of how something will end up, we may instead not attempt because the result could be terrible.

Taking a stab at something new turns into a gamble.

Where Does Dread of Progress Come From?

The apprehension about change can originate from youth encounters, familial perspectives, individual standpoints, current circumstances, and how individuals are customized.

For instance, assuming that somebody experiences childhood in a family that takes a negative perspective and is loaded with criticism could raise dread and tension over having a go at a new thing. This is remarkably normal if your folks have managed injury, misuse, or neediness. Their encounters might have made a perspective that advances the feeling that all ways are hazardous and loaded up with terrible results. Like that, you have become customized to be exhausted and pessimistic too.

It becomes simpler to stay with what is known.

Moreso, people are adapted and usually customized to get a kick out of the chance to be in charge. It's transformative. In this way, the apprehension about change results from nature and support.

That being said, it very well may be overseen and modified.

It takes work to understand that eventually, throughout everyday life, everything was once an unexplored world. It makes a grit and moves to push toward a way of energy and valuable results. That is why pursuing a mentality that can welcome and embrace change is so important.

Ways Of defeating the Apprehension of Change

Here are reliable ways of assisting you with conquering the feeling of dread toward change. Everybody needs their training to track down the right arrangement. However, these thoughts are a decent beginning spot to find what works for you:

1. Attempt hypnotherapy:

The apprehension about change is woven in one's mind. Hypnotherapy can assist with finding where it stems and abrogates the inclination.

2. More treatments:
There are likewise various sorts of treatments that can assist with freeing the trepidation from change. Bunch treatment, talk treatment, neuro-semantic treatment, conduct treatment, and recording your sentiments are ways you can utilize treatment to help with conquering this fear.

3. Embrace change and weakness:
You are weak places where you can confront your feelings of trepidation. It's tolerating that you might not have control, yet you can survive and deal with any situation or circumstance you face. At the point when you can invite change (with all it's likely great and terrible), you can recover a feeling of force.

4. Split things up into more modest pieces:
You don't need to work within limits. For instance, you might have numerous parts of your life that will require change — from picking your major to securing the correct position, going to the web or conventional school, choosing a soul mate, and that's only the tip of the iceberg. Attempting to confront this large number of changes immediately is, without a doubt, overpowering. Separate things into more modest pieces. Along these lines, to pick your school major, begin by recording what you like to do and what you're keen on. Then, consider your future and what you might need as your calling. Then, you can move toward this choice reasonably and move toward settling on the decision.

5. Know your why:
By characterizing your motivation, you can reduce your apprehension about change. If you don't have the foggiest idea of what you need, then any choice can be startling; however, in the event that you initially comprehend your "why," when you need to decide or a change, you can inquire as to whether it will line up with your motivation. This can assist with killing choices that don't pursue accomplishing objectives.

6. Stay optimistic and plan for the most pessimistic scenario:
While you can't necessarily control for results, you can have plans. Understand how you will respond if something flops wretchedly so you can diminish the outcomes as much as expected. What's more, to keep an uplifting perspective, hold out for divine intervention because your positive energy can assist with making positive results.

7. Encircle yourself with allies:

Throughout everyday life, you'll constantly have pessimistic and optimistic individuals around you. Attempt to perceive pundits and skeptical individuals and calm their effect at the forefront of your thoughts. All things being equal, influence individuals in your day-to-day existence who proposition backing and help to direct you in the correct course.

8. Practice "What if" emphatically:

When we don't know what will occur, we default to the most pessimistic scenario situations. You can practice asking yourself, "imagine a scenario in which it ends up working?" to consider the possible great results that can happen. Along these lines, you can assist the apprehension about change with disappearing.

9. Practice reiteration:

Like a competitor's muscle memory, you can prepare your cerebrum to follow a way of positive input instead of an adverse criticism circle. You need to embrace change and help yourself remember every time you rolled out an improvement, it turned out to improve things. Like that, you can condition your mind to embrace change instead of fear it.

10. Reward yourself:

When you roll out an improvement, you need to track down ways of remunerating yourself. It doesn't need to be anything unmistakable. You can prepare your psyche to accept you're acquiring another positive prize, regardless of whether you are eliminating something from your life.

11. Pose the proper inquiries:

Ask yourself what you are so scared of before leaving on any change. You can then record the likely results and perspectives you dread most. From this rundown, you can do an exploration to moderate these outcomes. Understanding what you dread will permit you to beat the apprehension and move toward change judiciously.

12. Be available:

While the past can be an educator, you want to zero in on where you are currently to push ahead. Utilize the data you have in the present time and place to go with your choices in light of your circumstances. Living in what's to come is obscure and adds to the tension. Being in the now makes way for an open door.

The Phases of Progress and How to Deal with Them

All change works go through four stages.

1. Expectation:

This is where we guess what can occur from change. It feels energizing.

Embrace these affections however long they last, and try to help yourself remember them during the following stage. Record your motivation and how this change can assist you with accomplishing objectives. Like that, you can allude back to this when you go through any restless stages that follow.

2. Relapse:

When things turn out to be more awful before they improve. This is where tension and anxiety toward change back their heads.

This is the step at which you ought to rehearse the above to survive. You can record what possible results are, depend on emotionally supportive networks, and train your cerebrum to embrace change by permitting yourself to feel powerless.

3. Leap forward:

The advantages and positive results begin to show.

Reward yourself for rolling out the improvement and perceive how much good has come from everything!

4. Combination:

The new change turns into your standard.

Back to the same old thing. Keep in mind that you should confront change once more, and this change will soon turn into your new ordinary, as well.

Uniting Everything

It's a human instinct to fear change. Our cerebrums are wired to get a kick out of the chance to be in charge and realize what's going on and when it is working out. This is for endurance and insurance.

Be that as it may, life is eccentric. Like this, it's critical to figure out how to acknowledge the obscure and rehearse a positive mentality while moving toward change.

Eventually, everybody will encounter apprehension about change, so ideally, a portion of the above tips and deceives can assist with defeating such trepidation and lead you to make a move!

Squander Energy on Things They Have zero control over.

So frequently, we stress over every one of some unacceptable things. As opposed to zeroing in on getting ready for the storm, we squander energy wishing the disruption wouldn't come. Assuming we focused on the things we do have command over, we'd be vastly improved and ready for anything that life tosses our direction. Focus on the times when you're enticed to stress over something you have zero control over — like the options others make or how your rival acts — and give that energy to something more useful.

10 Demonstrated Ways Of Preparing Your Cerebrum to Quit Agonizing Over Things You Have no control over

If you're the individual who just can't quit stressing, it is about time you train your mind to stop zeroing in on things you have no control over.

Stressing is not something to be embarrassed about. It's a typical piece of our reality. We stress over many things regularly - how to cover the bills, how safe our children are at school, where to go on our next outing, or our partners' opinion of us. We even stress minor things like who unfriended or unfollowed us on Facebook, which superstar said a final farewell to whom, or how we have a messy hair day.

Notwithstanding, when stress becomes insane, it turns into an issue. The ongoing or inordinate concern will prompt emotional well-being issues.

Per the Public Foundation of Psychological well-being, tension confusion is the most common dysfunctional behavior in the US. Around 18% of the US populace, which means 40 million grown-ups matured 18 to 54, have been determined to have tension turmoil.

Many individuals believe that their concerns should stop, yet don't have the foggiest idea how. Could it be said that you are one of them?

The following are ten demonstrated ways of preparing your mind to quit agonizing over things you have no control over:

1. Acknowledge the things you can't change.

One reason we stress an excess is that we will generally zero in on issues that are impossible for us to address or things we have no control over. For instance, we are arranging a birthday festivity at the end of the week, and we stress over it regardless of whether it will rain. There's an opportunity for it to rain. Rather than stressing over it, why not be adaptable and have an elective arrangement? This will facilitate your concerns.

Tolerating the way you have no control over all will lift a great deal of weight from your shoulders and ultimately end your concern.

2. Try not to attempt to think about what's at the forefront of somebody's thoughts.

Sometimes we attempt to make our tale about what's happening in an individual's psyche regardless of whether we know it in reality. For instance, assuming that we offered something a smidgen off to a companion or partner that isn't deliberate, we expect they will be frantic at us. We then portray their angered countenances that we lose long rest periods because of stress. Notwithstanding, our feelings of dread are many times just minds.

Attempting to expect what's at the forefront of somebody's thoughts is often futile and a lost cause. Our psyche is equipped for making situations that are both misrepresented and, here and there, even dangerous. If we let our minds harp and fixate on these psychological pictures, our concerns will go on and on forever.

Rather than stressing, why not approach the individual promptly to understand what the person is honestly thinking? This will save you a difficult situation not too far off.

3. Invest more energy at the present.

Nothing wrong can be said with occasionally thinking back about the past, particularly assuming you are contemplating something that moves you. In any case, investing an excess of energy in the past can represent a few issues.

"At the point when you invest a lot of energy remembering the past to you then beginning taking care of your stresses over the future is simple. When you spend an excess of energy later on, it is likewise simple to move, cleared away by sad situations.

The wisest thing you can do is center your time and consideration on the current where you can conclude what works for you and complete what you need to do.

So embrace the here and now, get some margin to appreciate the experience, inhale, and appreciate what it brings to the table.

4. Relinquish control.

Once in a while, we tend to need to control everything. We maintain that everything should be painstakingly framed and followed, and on the off chance that things don't go as expected, we blow a gasket and stress. That's what we imagine on the off chance that things don't turn out well for us; all that will be a wreck, and turmoil will follow. Once in a while, due to stress, we even need to control how individuals act towards us or how they think. However, we as a whole realize this is unimaginable. We can never assume command over everything, even our concerns.

"Attempting to overwhelm stress lights tension and stress contemplations. 'At the point when you have an idea you could do without, your body answers by battling truly to control it and break from it. Furthermore, that escalates the idea,' LeJeune says.

So your objective is the inverse — to interfere with the desire to fortify your tension. It's to permit acknowledgment and care to enter, LeJeune writes in The Concern Trap." through 5 Moves toward Decreasing Concern and Nervousness.

Nature has its particular manner of curving things to the point that we are often left frightened on the off chance that we are not ready. When we comprehend that we are not accountable for the universe and figure out how to adjust, we will have fewer excuses for stressing out.

5. Try not to be vain.

Vanity is a typical reason for stress for many individuals, for the younger age, and, in any event, for more established individuals.

"We frequently stress over individuals' thought process of us. We stress interminably that we probably won't live up to society's assumptions; we stress over regardless of whether individuals will like us. With this psychological viewpoint, we begin to give an excessive amount of significance to our inner self; it implies we continually search for appreciation and the reverence of others. On the off chance that we don't get this appreciation, we begin to stress that we are not decent. If we can foster more prominent self-assurance and internal balance, then, at that point, we won't stress over what others accept or think.

"We really want to give less significance to the assessments of the world. Regardless of whether we get censured, we shouldn't stress since we shouldn't distinguish our self-esteem from the assessments of others. This isn't difficult to do expedite; at the same time, on the off chance that we can confine ourselves to decisions of others, we will acquire more prominent inward harmony and try not to stress over the general irrelevance of individuals' decisions." through Quit Stressing.

The best answer for conquering stress on the vanity is to not focus on others' opinions of you. This is the sort of thing we have zero control over. Foster a solid mental self-portrait by zeroing in on your best highlights and resources.

6. Converse with a companion.

When you stress over something, it is vital to have somebody to converse with so your concerns won't torment your psyche. On the off chance that you have a dear companion, examine with them what's happening. Simply the prospect that somebody is tuning in and understanding where you're coming from frequently facilitates your concern.

More often than not, in the wake of conversing with somebody, you will acknowledge in the end that what you're worried about is significantly too stressed over by any stretch of the imagination!

7. Move back from web-based entertainment.

Despite its many benefits, virtual entertainment is frequently the reason for our concerns. "Research demonstrates how virtual entertainment can make us sad and feeling insufficient from steady correlation — yet we want more. In a review, 55% of individuals revealed feeling "stressed or awkward" when they were away from Facebook or email."

Nonetheless, remaining associated with online entertainment additionally adds to our concerns. On Facebook, for instance, we see our old colleagues, companions, or family members posting about their lovely children, their family, their movements, their fantasy house, their optimal positions or organizations, and their victories. So we contrast ourselves with these individuals and frequently feel insufficient because we haven't arrived at that "level" yet. What we don't have any idea about, however, is that these individuals have issues as well. They will post beneficial things about their lives that make them seem like they have an ideal life.

So, if you feel like web-based entertainment causes you to feel unreliable and insufficient, now is the ideal time to step away. Take a stab at decreasing the time you're spending understanding posts. Try not to allow your life to spin around virtual entertainment and spotlight your world.

8. Record your concerns.

Composing or journaling is an excellent treatment. At the point when you're stressing, have a go at recording everything on paper. This training will quiet your nerves and gives you a few arrangements en route.

"Scientists found that recording your concerns worked best in the most restless understudies making a "level battleground" with their more sure partners. Understudies who were exceptionally restless about bringing tests that recorded their contemplations before the trial got a standard grade of B+, contrasted and the profoundly troubled understudies who didn't compose, who got a standard B-.

"Expounding on your concerns for 10 minutes before an impending test evened the odds with the end goal that those understudies who generally get generally restless during tests had the option to conquer their feelings of dread and perform up to their true capacity," Prof Beilock said." through Compose Away Your Concerns If You Need to Succeed.

9. Significantly impact your viewpoint.

"Energy streams where you concentrate. Comprehend that you can decide to zero in on particular as opposed to negative contemplations as you become more confident.

Continuously decide to be hopeful. Train your mind to be excellent as a cucumber and check out the positive side of things. The more sure you get, the more specific the outcomes will be.

10. Find the correct facts

Sometimes, we go through days stressing and acknowledge in the end that what we are agonizing over is false. This is a sad truth that presumably a ton of us have encountered.

"Individuals stress when they have wrong data or need more data. We should assume you had questions that a specific stomach hurt implies that you have a problematic sickness; in such a case conversing with a specialist can end your concerns immediately as you would find that you have been misguided. Try not to fall into the snare of gathering data from companions or erroneous sources, yet head for specialists.

More often than not, as you are given the entire picture, you will understand that there is no excellent explanation for stress.

Conclusion:

Even though stress is an exceptionally regular thing, more often than not, it is pointless. Consequently, you want to begin to prepare your mind to quit stressing over something you have no control over. This will save you a lot of cerebral pains. When you follow the things introduced above, ideally, you will want to limit or ultimately quit stressing and appreciate life more.

Stress Over Satisfying Others.

Many individuals say, "it doesn't matter at all to me others' thought process," yet frequently, that is a safeguard instrument intended to protect them from the hurt and agony related to dismissal. Accommodating people come in all structures. Here and there, you can detect one a pretty far, and at different times, their feeling of dread toward enraging others is well established. Doing and making statements that may not be met with favor takes mental fortitude, yet carrying on with real life expects you to live as per your qualities, even when your decisions aren't well known.

Instructions to Quit Being a People-Pleaser

People-pleaser is known for taking the necessary steps to fulfill others. While being benevolent and supportive is, by and large, something to be thankful for, going excessively far to satisfy others can leave you feeling drained, pushed, and restless.

This article covers the characteristics of an accommodating person, the reasons for this way of behaving, and the pessimistic effect it can have. It additionally examines tips to assist you with halting putting others before your prosperity and guarantee that you deal with your requirements.

What Is a People Pleaser.

Human satisfying includes putting another person's necessities in front of your own. Accommodating people are susceptible to others and are frequently viewed as pleasant, supportive, and kind. Be that as it may, accommodating people might experience difficulty pushing for themselves, prompting an unsafe example of generosity or self-disregard.

Human satisfaction is related to a character quality known as "sociology," or feeling excessively worried about satisfying others and procuring their endorsement as a method for keeping up with relationships.2 This conduct can be a side effect of a psychological wellness condition like

Nervousness or misery

Avoidant behavioral condition

Marginal behavioral condition (BPD)

Codependency or ward behavioral condition

Signs You May Be A People Pleaser.

Various qualities accommodating people will quite often share. Here are a few signs that you may be an accommodating person:

You struggle with saying "no."

You are engrossed with what others could think.

You feel regretful when you tell individuals "no."

You dread that turning individuals down will make them think you are mean or egotistical.

You consent to things you could do without or do something you would instead not do.

You battle with sensations of low confidence.

You believe individuals should like you and feel that getting things done for them will procure their endorsement.

You're continuously telling individuals you're grieved.

You assume the fault in any event when something isn't your shortcoming.

You never have any extra energy since you continuously get things done for others.

You disregard your necessities to get things done for other people.

You claim to concur with individuals even though you feel unexpectedly.

A people pleaser will generally be excellent at checking out what others are feeling. They are additionally commonly compassionate, insightful, and mindful. These positive characteristics may likewise accompany an unfortunate mental self-view, need to assume command, or propensity to overachieve.

While individuals could portray you as a provider or liberal individual, when you're an accommodating person, all of this work to keep others blissful may leave you feeling depleted and pushed.

Causes

Stop being a people-pleaser; it's critical to see a portion of the justifications for why you may be taking part in this sort of conduct. Various variables could assume a role, including:

Lacking self-confidence: Sometimes, individuals participate in satisfying human behavior because they don't esteem their longings and necessities. Because of an absence of self-assurance, accommodating people require outer approval, and they might feel that getting things done for others will prompt endorsement and acknowledgment.

Frailty: In different cases, individuals could attempt to satisfy others since they stress that others won't care for them if they don't exceed all expectations in fulfilling them.

Hairsplitting: Here and there, individuals maintain that everything should be "just so," including how others think and feel.

Previous encounters: Excruciating, troublesome, or horrible encounters may likewise assume a part. For instance, individuals who have encountered misuse may attempt to satisfy others and be pretty much as pleasing as conceivable to try not to set off harmful conduct in others.

The inspiration to help others can sometimes be a type of selflessness. An individual could need to ensure that others have the assistance they require. Human satisfaction can be a method for feeling approved or loved in different cases. By fulfilling what individuals are, they think they are helpful and esteemed.

Impacts of Being A Yes Person.

Human satisfaction isn't something terrible. Being a concerned and caring individual is a significant piece of keeping up with solid associations with friends and family. It turns into an issue, in any case, on the off chance that you are attempting to win endorsement to support feeble confidence or if you are seeking after the satisfaction of others to the detriment of your close-to-home prosperity.

On the off chance that you are committing all of your opportunity to help others to make them blissful and win their endorsement, you could encounter a portion of the accompanying outcomes.

Outrage and Dissatisfaction

While you could appreciate helping, you likewise will undoubtedly encounter dissatisfaction when you do things hesitantly or out of commitment. These sentiments can prompt a pattern of aiding somebody, feeling distraught at them for making use, and afterward feeling remorseful or sorry for yourself.

One investigation discovered that individuals with a solid need to satisfy others were likewise more inclined to gorge in social situations.

Nervousness and Stress

Endeavors to keep others cheerful can make your physical and mental assets dainty. Attempting to oversee everything can leave you tormented with pressure and uneasiness, which can inconveniently affect your well-being.

Assisting others with canning has various psychological wellness benefits.5 Yet, not allowing for yourself implies you could wind up encountering the negative well-being results of overabundance stress.

Drained Determination

Committing the entirety of your energy and mental assets toward ensuring that others are implied, you are less inclined to have the purpose and determination to handle your objectives.

Some exploration recommends that resolution and discretion might be restricted resources.6 Assuming you are utilizing your psychological assets to ensure that others have what they need or need, it could imply that you essentially have minimal left to give to your requirements.

Absence of Legitimacy

A Yes person will frequently conceal their necessities and inclinations to oblige others. This can cause you to feel as though you are not carrying on with your life; it might leave you feeling as though you don't know yourself by any stretch of the imagination.

Concealing your actual sentiments makes it hard for others to get to know the genuine you. Self-divulgence is significant in any cozy relationship, yet it isn't successful if you're not revealing your actual self.7

More fragile Connections

Assuming you are investing every one of your amounts of energy into ensuring that you measure up to others' assumptions, you might discover yourself feeling angry. While individuals could see the value in your giving nature, they may likewise start to underestimate your generosity and mindfulness.

Individuals may not understand they are exploiting you. All they know is that you are continuously able to help, so they have most likely that you'll show up at whatever point you're required. They may not see the means by which meager you are extended and how overcommitted you may be.

I am being Decent versus Being an Accommodating person.

There is a differentiation between getting things done to be great and doing something since you're accommodating. Individuals frequently do decent stuff for a scope of reasons: to feel better, to help, to return some help, or to procure some help. If you're accomplishing something since you are anxious about the possibility that you'll be detested or dismissed assuming that you say "no," there are areas of strength for that human satisfaction is working.

Tips to Stop Human Satisfying

Luckily, there are means that you can take to quit being an accommodating person and figure out how to adjust your longing to satisfy others without forfeiting your own.

Lay out Limits

It's critical to know your cutoff points, lay out clear limits, and afterward impart those cutoff points. Be clear and explicit about the thing you're willing to take on. Assuming it appears as though somebody is requesting excessively, let them know that it's over the limits of what you will do and that you will not have the option to help.

There are alternate ways of limiting your day-to-day existence to assist with reigning in your kin's satisfying propensities. For instance, you could accept calls at specific times to draw certain lines when you can talk.

It could make sense that you are just accessible for a particular timeframe. This can be useful because it guarantees that you have control of what you will do and when you will make it happen.

Begin Little

It tends to be challenging to roll out an unexpected improvement, so starting by standing up for yourself in little ways is frequently more straightforward. Changing standards of conduct can be troublesome.

By and large, it would help if you retrain yourself and chip away at assisting individuals around you to grasp your cutoff points.

Along these lines, it tends to be helpful, to begin with, little advances that assist you with working your approach to being, to a lesser degree, an accommodating person. Begin by expressing no to more modest solicitations, take a stab at offering your viewpoint about something minor, or request something that you want.

For instance, take a stab at expressing no to a text demand. Then, at that point, move gradually up to telling individuals "no" face to face. Practice in various settings or circumstances, for example, while conversing with sales reps, requesting at a café, or in any event, while managing colleagues.

Each time you remove a little step from being an accommodating person, you'll acquire more prominent certainty that will assist you with assuming back command over your life.

Put forth Objectives and Boundaries

Consider where you need to invest your energy. Who would you like to help? What objectives would you say you are attempting to achieve? Realizing your needs can assist you with deciding if you have the opportunity and energy to dedicate to something.

If something is draining your energy or taking a lot of your time, do whatever it may take to resolve the issue. As you work on defining those limits and expressing no to things you would prefer not to do, you'll find that you have additional opportunities to commit to the things that mean quite a bit.

Attempt Positive Self-Talk

If you begin to feel overpowered or enticed to buckle, develop your determination with good self-talk. Advise yourself that you have the right to possess energy for yourself. Your objectives are significant, and you shouldn't feel committed to offering your considerable investment on things that don't give you pleasure.

Slow down for Time

At the point when somebody requests some help, let them know you want a chance to consider it. Saying "OK" immediately can leave you feeling committed and overcommitted, yet taking as much time as necessary to answer a solicitation can allow you to assess it and choose if it's something you genuinely desire to do. Before you settle on a choice, ask yourself:

What amount of time will this require?

Is this something I truly need to do?
Do you have the opportunity and energy to make it happen?
How focused am I going to be assuming I say "OK?"
Research has likewise found that even a brief delay increases decision-production accuracy before settling on a decision.8 By giving yourself a second, you'll be better ready to precisely choose if it is something you have the craving and time to take on.

Evaluate the Solicitation

One more move toward defeating being an accommodating person is to search for signs that others are attempting to exploit your liberality. Are there individuals who generally appear to need something from you yet are out of nowhere inaccessible if you want them to give back? Or, on the other hand, genuinely do specific individuals appear to be mindful of your liberal nature and ask because they realize that you would say "no?"

Assuming it seems like you're being maneuvered toward getting things done, carve out an opportunity to survey what is going on and conclude how you need to deal with the solicitation. Be firm and clear for habitual perpetrators or individuals who continue to demand that you ought to help.

Try not to Rationalize

Being immediate when you say "no" and abstain from faulting different commitments or rationalizing your powerlessness to participate is significant." When you explain why you can't follow through with something, you give others a method for punching holes in your reason. Or on the other hand, you might be allowing them the opportunity to change their solicitation to guarantee that you can, in any case, do what they are inquiring about.

Take a stab at utilizing an unequivocal tone when you decline something and fight the temptation to add pointless insights concerning your thinking. Advise yourself that "no" is a finished sentence.

Recollect that Connections Require Compromise

A solid, sound relationship includes a specific level of correspondence. Assuming one individual is continuously giving and the other is constantly taking, it frequently implies that one individual is doing without things they need to guarantee that the other has what they need.

Regardless of whether you appreciate pleasing others, it is essential to recall that they should likewise be doing whatever it may take to offer you as a trade-off.

Help When You Need to Help

You don't have to quit any pretense of being kind and insightful. Those are helpful characteristics that can add areas of strength for connections. The key is to inspect your inspirations and goals. Try not to do things simply because you dread dismissal or need the endorsement of others.

However, continue to do valuable things according to your preferences. Thoughtfulness doesn't request consideration or prizes — it requires a longing to improve things for someone else.

Mess up the same way Again and again.

It'd be ideal for advancing enough from each slip-up that we'd ensure never to rehash that equivalent misstep two times. However, we're inclined to rehash similar mix-ups some of the time. Gaining from our slip-ups requires lowliness and a readiness to search for new procedures to turn out to be better. Intellectually resilient individuals don't conceal their slip-ups or rationalize them. They transform their missteps into valuable open doors for self-development.

How To Stop Making The Same Mistakes Over And Over

The road to success is often tricky, fraught with missteps and unforeseen challenges.

It's rare for a person to travel straight from start to success in whatever they are undertaking, whether building on a career or attaining personal development goals.

The road gets a bit trickier if you make the same mistakes over and over because you essentially lose time while spinning your wheels looking for traction.

How can we avoid that? How can we stop making the same mistakes again and again? Let's look at a relatively simple, direct strategy that anyone can put into practice.

1. Forgive yourself for making a mistake.

The relationship that people have with failure is not an accurate reflection of what failure means. The reality is that most endeavours in the world fail, and they fail for an infinite number of reasons.

Sometimes the timing of the endeavour is off; occasionally, when an idea is not marketed or promoted well, a person lacks the skills or necessary resources to find success, and sometimes people give up before they ever really get going.

Failure is not a bad word. Failure means you tried something, and it didn't work out. Yes, the consequences of a failure can be harsh and sometimes life-changing, but you still need to forgive yourself for your failures.

People are imperfect. Mistakes will happen. They are a part of the lives of every single person in this world.

It's what you do about those failures that matter. Be kind to yourself. Forgive yourself. Try again.

2. Identify the mistake that has been made.

The key to solving any problem is to understand what the problem is in the first place.

I like to take some time to think about a mistake I've made or a recent failure and write it at the top of a piece of paper.

I need to form a concrete idea of what the mistake was that I made and articulate it because that will allow me to work backwards from the error to see how I got there.

3. Identify what a successful resolution will look like.

The next step I take is to identify what a successful resolution will look like.

On my sheet of paper, I write out what I feel would be a successful resolution. What is your goal? What are you aiming to achieve?

Write that down, but understand that success may not be precise as you envision, so you don't want to get too wrapped up in the idea of this success.

Things may change. You may eventually find that your standards for success were off because of a lack of knowledge or experience about the item.

You may also find that your efforts take you to a place you like and enjoy but isn't necessarily what you envisioned. Shifting your goal when you get new, the relevant information is okay.

4. Trace the route of your decision-making that brought you to the mistake.

At this point, it is time to reverse-engineer the route that brought you to your mistake. You do this by asking questions. Questions such as:

What bad decisions did I make from when I started pursuing that success to when it finally came apart?

What good decisions did I make that I can incorporate in future attempts?

Did I lack knowledge? Information? Experience? Perspective?

Was my goal narrow? Too broad?

Is there a point where I could have made different decisions that would have brought me to the resolution I was looking for?

What role did I play in this mistake?

What external factors negatively impacted my pursuit of this goal?

How could I have lessened the impact of the pitfalls and shortcomings I experienced?

5. Research other methods for attaining the successful resolution you're looking for.

The great thing about the advance in technology is that we now have the internet to dig into for additional information.

Take some time to look for quality information on your goal and the processes involved in attaining that goal. This will give you a huge pool of knowledge to draw from in trying to plan out your new course of action.

The additional perspective will help you determine if your goal is reasonable and attainable. You may find that it needs to be reevaluated or that you need to shoot for a smaller goal on your much larger path.

6. Develop a strategy and course of action to reach your successful resolution.

It's time to develop a strategy. What elements are going to bring you to a successful resolution? What pitfalls do you need to avoid? What steps do you need to take, starting from the very first to what you'd consider your success?

Map these steps out on your sheet of paper as a step-by-step course of action. Consider this the first draft of your strategy.

As you reach each step, you will find that it may not look exactly as you anticipated. You will likely encounter unforeseen problems or setbacks you must navigate and overcome.

Use the problem-solving approach presented in Step 5 if you are having a difficult time – research, research, research!

7. Be willing to try again with your new and different strategy.

The most crucial step in pursuing success is to be willing to accept failure and try again. Your new plan might not work out. That's just how it goes sometimes. Depending on what you're doing, you may need to change your strategy and try again.

The upside is that you gain a fair amount of experience as you work through this process. The downside, of course, is that no one likes to feel like they are failing or not making due progress.

The only real strategy is to grin and bear it, keep pushing forward, and adjust your system, but don't lose your goal. You can overcome and succeed!

Regarding Therapy.

Sometimes, a person may be making the same mistakes for reasons that are out of their control.

Life is hard and painful for many, and surviving it can create unhealthy coping mechanisms that serve the person well to endure whatever negative situations they are going through but are toxic and destructive in healthier cases.

Suppose you are having a hard time mentally or emotionally. In that case, it is a worthwhile investment to talk to a certified therapist about the situation because they may be able to help you overcome those hurdles by helping you address the root causes of those mistakes.

It's not unusual for people with depression, anxiety, or other mental health issues to make the same mistakes over and over. Unwell thought processes can mess with our ability to reason, accurately judge situations, and follow through on our plans.

A certified therapist may be able to point you to strategies and paths that other people who have faced similar changes have used to attain their success if you find that you're not able to do it on your own.

Chapter 3 20 Small Habits That Will Increase Your Mental Attitude

Everybody needs to begin the year solidly. However, it's ending on a good note that is likewise significant. Numerous goals and objectives are never reached because we become involved with what's going on in our lives and haven't fostered the psychological solidarity to push ourselves along when the energy from the New Year wears off.

Nonetheless, a great deal of getting yourself to your objectives and outperforming them is tied with being significant areas of intellectual strength when those hard minutes hit. Discipline is grown, so it's determination and the persistent capacity to pursue incredible decisions toward what you need. Remember not to forfeit what you genuinely need for some delight now.

Being intellectually more grounded doesn't mean it must be intense drudgery; the following are some tips and deceives that can help you. I very much like to be more grounded. Indeed it would be best if you did activities to keep the muscles solid, develop mental fortitude, and do exercises to build those propensities and convictions.

One ideal way to develop mental fortitude is to track down propensities over the day to keep your energy high, outlook good, and assist with creating tendencies and abilities which will help push you ahead and give you a decent outlook on the thing you're doing. In the meantime, you're developing mental fortitude in a way that won't leave you feeling depleted and overpowered.

Put yourself in a position for an intellectually more grounded and more joyful year by applying a couple of these tips:

1. Make Your Bed

You're, as of now, getting things done and starting very well when you make your bed first thing. Recollect the idiom, "The condition of your bed is the condition of your head?" There is a lot of truth to it. In comparison, it might appear like a little step has colossal advantages.

Research shows individuals who make their beds daily are generally more joyful with their lives, more valuable, and have a more grounded deep satisfaction and achievement in their day for every errand. This easily overlooked detail makes you prone to complete tasks immediately in the first part of the day. One is undertaking down before you've even cleaned your teeth; what an extraordinary inclination!

2. Direct Decent Sentiments toward Yourself Day to day

Promise to eliminate the negative self-talk and siphon up the decent things you tell yourself. You might feel ludicrous right away as you become your own team promoter in your mind, yet contemplate how extraordinary you'll feel as you settle on increasingly firm conclusions about your life. Those equivalent choices will keep you pushing toward your objective.

Be careful; negative considerations can sneak their direction rapidly; when you get them, remember them as false (regardless of whether you need to express them without holding back) and supplant them with a positive idea.

3. Record Something Extraordinary About Every Day

You can keep it in a container, a diary, a shoe box, or any place you need; however, record something extraordinary every day. This makes appreciation in your life.

Toward the year's end, you'll have the option to plunk down and glance back at the positive things you've encountered and achieved, rather than just the difficulties or challenging situations which made you need to surrender.

4. Record the Positive Parts of Every Experience.

Life is a ton about point of view. Adjust your point of view, and you can transform yourself.

Rather than complaining and being furious or disheartened (enjoying negative self-talk) concerning any difficulties that might arise, develop your cheerful mental fortitude by recording positive perspectives and things you could gain from the problems. Make an honest effort to view something as thankful about each day.

5. Practice Careful Bliss While Driving

Care is tied in with being at the time. To become familiar with being cheerful, working on being carefully blissful.

Take an occasion, second, or memory when you are feeling much better, and allow yourself to enjoy the inclination. Take a gander at how it sits in your body, how your contemplations change, how your body changes, and what it seems like; check whether there are any tones it might feel like.

Do you have at least some idea of what's absent in your everyday routine that keeps you away from experiencing life without limit? End the Existence Appraisal For nothing and figure out what parts of life require your prompt consideration and what you want to carry on with the existence you need.

Invest some energy in your cheerful state of mind. Toward its finish, notice the sensation of bliss and euphoria, it comes from you, and it unexpectedly shows up when you are in care at the time.

6. Work on Being Your Own Closest companion Everyday

This is an excellent method for becoming intellectually more grounded because it helps us to depend on ourselves and not need others to get us since we can do it without anyone's help.

Whenever something isn't going very as expected, or you begin to affront or reprimand yourself, stop and inquire:

"Could I allow my dearest companion to treat me along these lines?" or "Could I treat my dearest companion along these lines?"

The response is most likely no, and it's brilliant to adore yourself so much, while possibly not more, than you love your closest companion.

7. Work on Saying "No" without Clarification

As a general public, we've concluded someplace along the lines that we must have a justification for saying no, and not having any desire to accomplish something is certainly not a sufficient explanation. If you wind up in that thought process, toss it out.

Figure out how to say no. You don't need to clarify your activities or approve your choices for anybody about why you would instead not follow through with something.

8. Practice 20 Minutes of Taking care of oneself day to day

It doesn't make any difference what your identity is or what you do, on the off chance that you don't require some investment to profoundly focus on yourself, you'll ultimately run your well dry and not have the option to adore and focus on everyone around you.

Taking care of oneself can be as perplexing as having a nail trim or spa day or as essential as securing yourself in the restroom for five minutes to have some alone time. It doesn't make any difference what it is; ensure you make some space or do exercises that leave you feeling full and cheerful.

Investigate The 5-Step Manual for Taking care of oneself for Occupied Individuals.

9. Do a Side interest or Action every day Which Gives You Pleasure

This is an incredible type of taking care of oneself. Check whether you can't find a side interest or Action you appreciate because it encourages you.

As you become more confident and capable, you'll find how certainty and self-conviction will pool over into different parts of your life. The positive talk you use and the delight you find in your leisure activity will make you intellectually more grounded as you tackle the more challenging parts of your picked objective.

10. Put forth an Objective to Practice More Appreciation and Less Whining

Becoming involved with the pattern of grumbling can make it hard to be near, yet it can truly take a cost to your emotional well-being. Rather than continually griping about a circumstance, attempt and view something as thankful.

11. Put forth an Objective for something like 8 Hours of Rest an Evening

This is immense! You've seen little youngsters fly off the handle when they are excessively worn out. Grown-ups are the same way; we don't, for the most part, wind up ultimately dropped on our supper plate. When you're excessively drained, you make unfortunate choices, your psychological strength goes down, your rational brain transforms into a 6-year-old's, and your body answers by increasing pressure chemicals.

Focus on rest this year to assist you intellectually with your remaining areas of strength. At least eight hours is fundamental, on the off chance that you're any competitor, as much as possible. Assuming you're anxious, ensure you are giving yourself adequate opportunity to rest and unwind before nodding off to permit your body to boost the dozing hours.

12. Put forth an Objective to Eat Clean Food Day to day.

A new examination shows the connection between your stomach well-being and your state of mind, and something which straightforwardly connects with your stomach well-being is the food you put in your body.

like any food sensitivities, grains, dairy, and liquor, you can lessen the weight on your stomach-related framework. A better stomach-related framework implies fewer days off and more energy and can further develop side effects of dejections and uneasiness.

Attempt to shop the external edge of the staple story and eat just the food you make. Learn metal about clean eating here: What Is Spotless Eating (Fundamental Tips + Clean Eating Feast Plan)

13. Slice Your Web-based Entertainment Time Down the middle

We will generally do our absolute best via online entertainment, and this can wind up with us attempting to contrast our lives with the features reel of someone else's life. Doing so can leave you having a horrendous and discontent outlook on where you are throughout everyday life and the extraordinary things you've achieved. It can likewise make you fail to remember the number of extraordinary lives you that touch over the day by being the astounding individual you are.

A portion of your online entertainment time and invest the energy reconnecting with individuals you love, perusing a book, or rehearsing the side interest you appreciate. Whatever you choose to occupy the time with, ensure it's something that lifts you.

14. Set up somewhere around Three Moving Statements to day to day Peruse

When circumstances become complicated, and you feel like you're not gaining ground, inspiring words can go far toward keeping you on target.

Get some margin to post a couple of moving statements or pictures (perhaps a dream board) someplace you'll see it consistently. Uplifting messages and inspiration can go a long when you're in a terrible spot.

15. Imagine Your Objectives for 10 Minutes every day

Carve out the opportunity to picture the final product of your objectives and the difficulties you'll in the middle.

Take note of your objective, and attempt to painstakingly anticipate your approach to accomplishing your goal. The Visionaries' Manual for Making a move And Arriving at Your Objective can assist you with doing this. A free aide can help you plan and adjust your regular activities to your objective.

Work on imagining how you will tackle likely issues. See yourself where you need to be, and feel the way that extraordinary it feels to achieve your objectives.

16. Relinquish Individuals Satisfying Inclinations

With an end goal to be a decent individual, we frequently overstretch ourselves and focus on things we genuinely don't have any desire to do.

Embrace the way that you can't satisfy everybody. Relinquish the need to let others' bliss and objectives overrule what's best for you, your well-being, and your joy.

17. Set a Month to monthly Financial plan Which Incorporates Something Fun

Anything good times ought to do. It doesn't need to be enormous. It very well may be purchasing another shirt, heading out to the film, or getting yourself the most loved bubble shower, which will cause you to grin and feel fantastic when you come into contact with it.

Whether lighting your new candle or absorbing a tub with your number one air pocket shower, let yourself partake in a little lavish expenditure consistently or scarcely any weeks.

18. Quit Enjoying Connections or Exercises Which Channel your Energy

Go where you're praised. Do things that leave you feeling cheerful. Make yourself intellectually more grounded by building positive connections and relinquishing harmful ones.

Relinquishing poisonous connections or spots is difficult, be that as it may, you need to commit to being more grounded earnestly. Without the psychological and close-to-home channel, you'll track down additional energy and more joy over your day.

19. Cut "Ought to" from Your Jargon

Contemplate when the last time you figured you ought to follow through with something. It wasn't precisely a tomfoolery and energizing idea, was it?

"Ought to," for the most part, accompanies genuine convictions, weighty obligation, and seldom a sensation of satisfaction. "Ought to" tends to accompany self-analysis and cruel judgment, neither of which support the establishment you're assembling this year to become intellectually more grounded.

Rather than utilizing "ought to," re-state your sentence into something you anticipate doing. For example, "I might want to be intellectually more grounded." or "I might want to be truly better."

20. Diary for Three Pages or Five Minutes Morning As well as Night

Assuming you decide to diary in the first part of the day, expound on your fantasies, dump every one of your concerns or worries on the page, to imaginatively communicate anything that might have previously concerned you. It's likewise a terrific method for recording your objectives and motivations for the afternoon, getting an inclination for what you need to witness, and an activity plan.

Assuming you decide to diary around evening time, loosen up everything that might have worried you, and commend everything you did well.

Regardless of what approach you require this year, recollect:

With a predictable positive practice, you can fortify your psychological muscles; over the long haul, you'll become intellectually more grounded!

www.ingramcontent.com/pod-product-compliance
Lightning Source LLC
Chambersburg PA
CBHW050310220526
45465CB00005B/1925